Ukulele
Chords, Exercises

Frederick Johnson
Copyright © 2019 Frederick Johnson
All rights reserved.

FREDERICK JOHNSON

Ukulele 101: Chords, Exercises & Techniques

WELCOME

A&M Books

FREDERICK JOHNSON

Contents:

1. Introduction to the Ukulele (1)

2. Reading Tablature (13)

3. Chords (23)

4. Strumming & Picking (39)

5. Technique 1: Pull Offs & Hammer-ons (45)

6. Technique 2: Soloing in C (53)

7. Technique 3: Barring (71)

8. Technique 4: Fifth & Seventh Chords (75)

FREDERICK JOHNSON

UKULELE 101
Chords, Exercises & Techniques

Essential Ukulele Chords

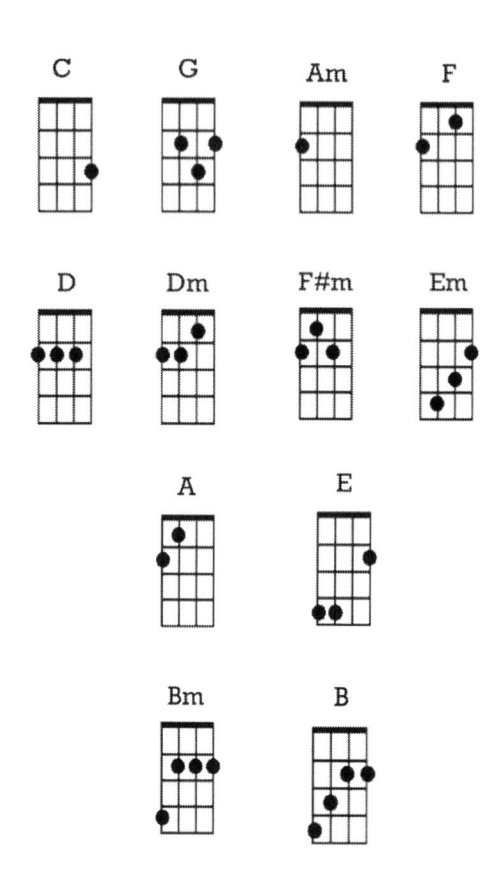

Introduction

Welcome to the ukulele and let me start by saying well done and a massive congratulations for choosing what Jake Shimabukuro (the world's most successful ukulele player) called the instrument of peace. Indeed how right he was and soon, you'll see just why the ukulele has become the most popular instrument to learn. These days, you find a lot of tutorials and lessons on the internet but what you won't find there is an in depth guide from day one to explain to you all the basics of the ukulele and give you step by step tuition. That is what this book is for: to provide you with an insightful and easy peasy method of playing the ukulele from the moment you open the box and hold the instrument in your hands for the very first time.

In this chapter, you will be given an introduction to your instrument. This involves a breakdown of the individual parts that make up the ukulele, some basic maintenance tips and preparing you to start strumming away.

What is a ukulele?

We will start by giving an overview of what a ukulele actually is. Many falsely believe that the ukulele is related to the guitar and therefore is part of the guitar family. Others believe that the ukulele is a stand alone instrument whereby it is unique as a construction and no other instruments like it exist. ***This is also a false misconception.***

The truth is that the ukulele is a family of instruments. The uke comes in four sizes: soprano, concert, tenor and baritone. With the increase in demand for stringed instrument production and with advances in recent luthier technology, new hybrids have also emerged such as the guitarlele which is a six string ukulele. This instrument was designed to help guitarists make an easy transition to the ukulele without actually having to learn the ukulele since the instrument has the same intonation as a guitar but tuned a fifth higher. The bass ukulele is another such hybrid. Nevertheless, the chances are that if you're starting the ukulele, you own a soprano since this is the most common kind. Psst… we think it's the best kind too. So let us now take a look at the different parts of the ukulele and what each component is for.

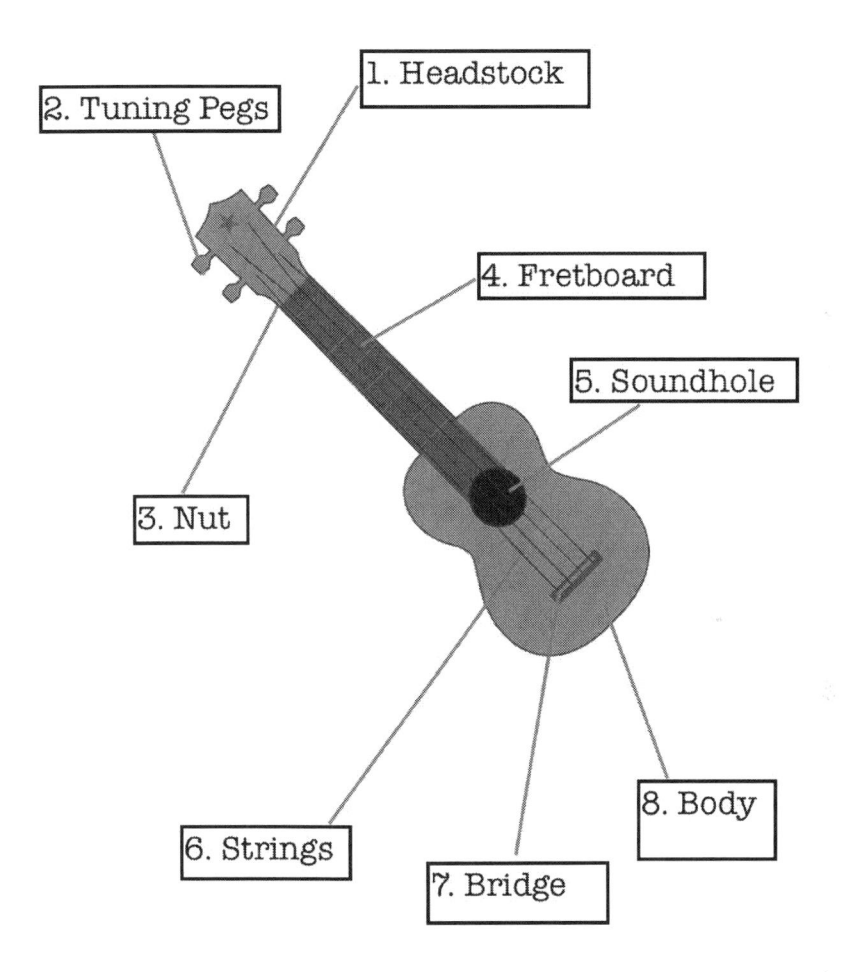

1. Headstock
2. Tuning Pegs
3. Nut
4. Fretboard
5. Soundhole
6. Strings
7. Bridge
8. Body

———————————Index———————————

1. Headstock

The function of the headstock is to contain the tuning pegs and to balance the ukulele's weight appropriately for an overall accurate intonation.

The headstock is a fragile part of the instrument which you should avoid knocking or hitting at all costs. This point cannot be emphasised enough. Since ukuleles are delicate in that they are smaller than most stringed instruments and have a tighter neck and string tension, even a single heavy knock can cause severe or even permanent damage to the instrument. Such damage can vary from your ukulele no longer staying in tune to a dented neck or even fret and nut problems. Any of these will cost you a lot of money, especially since ukulele repair is a niche field which not all guitar luthiers may be able to pull off successfully. It's best to take precautionary measures and look after your instrument. Purchase a gig bag or case for all transportation.

2. Tuning Pegs

There are four tuning pegs on the ukulele, one for each string. Ukulele tuning pegs are extremely sensitive and so when you are tuning your instrument, especially if you got your instrument new with no setup and loose strings, be extremely cautious as ukulele strings snap HARD if you tune incorrectly and are careless. Tune each peg slowly, turning them progressively - never in quick motions. Since guitars have longer necks than ukuleles, you can afford to tune in swift motions. Ukuleles are smaller and have a shorter distance between the strings and the headstock. Therefore, they tighten quickly. Bear this in mind when first tuning your new instrument.

3. Nut

The nut is often overlooked and some players do not take into consideration just how pivotal this little bit of material really is. The nut is the linking point between the strings, bridge and headstock. It contains four individual slits where the strings sit on. Damage to the nut is as bad as damage to the headstock, if not worse. What you must appreciate as a ukulele player is that while the nut seems futile, those individually spaced slits have been measured apart in a precise way down to the last millimetre. It is actually one of the most strenuous and laborious aspects of the craftsmanship that goes into fabrication of the instrument. When replacing strings, take your time and if you are ever unsure, have them replaced by your local music shop. Better to be safe than sorry.

4. Fretboard

The fretboard is the actual part of the instrument that your notation is played on. If you are right-handed, your left hand navigates this part of the ukulele. Ensure the frets (individually lined notes) are not sharp and are smooth. If there are any issues, make sure to address them professionally before playing as injuries are frequent in poorly constructed and set up ukuleles. Most guitar stores will be able to sort out minor issues. The fretboard sits on the neck which your hand grasps as you play.

5. Soundhole

The sound hole is pretty self explanatory. It's where sound emits out of the instrument when played. On acoustic guitars, it's where many people accidentally drop their picks into (*'plectrum'* for our lovely British and Australian readers). Nonetheless, be sure that nothing is inside the sound hole as this can impair performance and the overall sound of your ukulele.

6. Strings

Let's now talk about the strings of the ukulele. Similar to classical guitars, ukuleles use nylon or gut strings. We will talk specifically about the tuning of the ukulele in the next section of the book. Be aware that your strings should never feel too tight agains the fretboard of the ukulele. There should be an ease where you are able to press down on each fret and bend the strings a little bit. A maintenance tip is to purchase a guitar cleaning kit. These are inexpensive and usually contain conditioner. Keeping your strings clean is essential for hygiene and a crisp sounding instrument. Alternatively, use a duster and dab a small amount of water on a tea towel to regularly clean your fretboard and strings.

7. Bridge

The bridge is what holds the strings in place on the opposite end of the ukulele to the headstock. Don't mess around with this part of the ukulele as much like the other components which involve maintaining correct string tension, it is extremely delicate. You might note that the strings are tied in a knot on the bridge and unlike guitars, there are no pinned 'slots' in the bridge where you can insert strings into easily. This means that changing strings is not something you should try at home unless you are proficient in ukulele string replacement. Ask a guitar or music shop to do this for you when you do eventually buy new strings.

8. Body

Finally, the most prominent feature of your ukulele: its body. Look after it and ensure to dust it from time to time. Dust culminates a lot on the body's outer rim, the headstock and on top of the strings. Just like with any part of the instrument, ensure no physical damage occurs on it and love your. instrument like you love any other personal expensive property.

Tuning Up

Now that we have covered the basics of the instrument, it's time to start playing. The key to all good performance is a well tuned ukulele. Ukulele tuning is similar to other four stringed instruments but is very unique as the second string (the C string) is lower in pitch than the other strings. This is rare in stringed fretted instruments.

Ukulele tuning looks like this:

G   C   E   A

In tablature form (which we will look at very shortly), it looks like this:

```
A|--------------------------------------------|
E|-----------------------------------------  -|
C|--------------------------------------------|
G|--------------------------------------------|
```

Tablature

On the previous page, you were shown what we call tablature. Tablature is the full word for what are often known as 'tabs'. This is far more commonly used these days. Tablature is sheet music for ukulele and other stringed instruments. It shows us what notes we have to play through numbers on different strings. In ukulele tabs, the G note (the lowest string which is also closest to you) is the bottom string, the C note the next one along and so on.

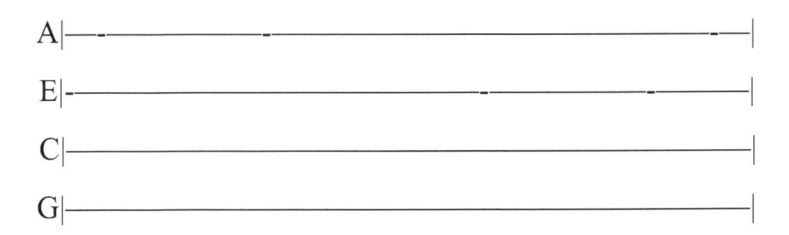

```
A|----                              -    -—|
E|-                                  -         -    |
C|                                              |
G|                                              |
```

The first thing that I would like you to do is to play each note openly: G to A.

In tablature, playing each note openly would look like this:

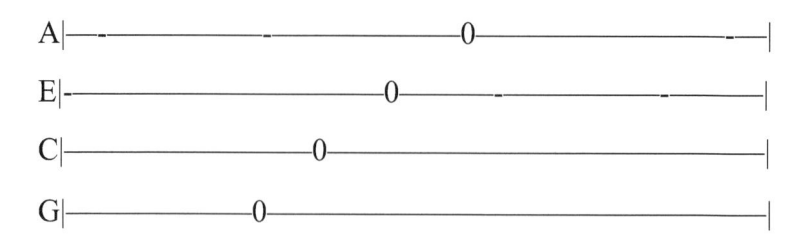

```
A|---------------------0--------------------|
E|-----------------0------------------------|
C|-------------0----------------------------|
G|---------0--------------------------------|
```

The reason for the 0 is that we aren't actually playing on a fret. The numbers demonstrate which fret we have to put our fingers on. An open string is always marked as a 0 in tablature.

It is time now for our first lesson. In this lesson, we will play a very simple pattern and you will see how it looks when we tab it out.

Lesson:

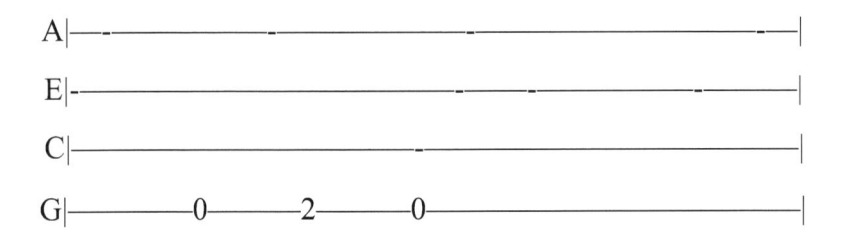

```
A|----                              -    -           -—|
E|-                                   -  -         -——|
C|                                 -                  —|
G|          0      2      0                           —|
```

For this lesson, you will be using the G string only.

Step 1: Play the open G string.

Step 2: Place your index finger (or middle finger) on the second fret of the G string and play it. The second fret is the second note away from the nut which is marked by the frets (the lines on the fretboard).

Step 3: Let go and play the G string open again.

We started with a 0 on the G string which marked the fact you played the string open. This was followed by the 2 which means you played the second fret and then we have a 0 again where a string is played openly. Now we are going to include other strings.

```
A|---------------------------------------------|
E|---------------------------------------------|
C|-------------5------2---------0--------------|
G|------0-----2--------------------------------|
```

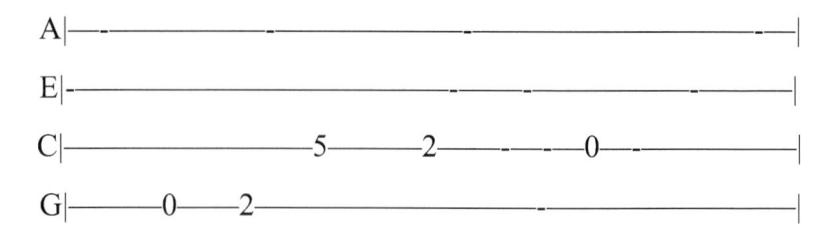

This might look intimidating at first but it really is something you are capable of performing with the knowledge you have acquired so far. Don't worry, I will guide you through.

Step 1: Start the tune by playing the G string open.

Step 2: Just like in the previous exercise, place your finger on the second fret of the G string.

Step 3: Now you want to place your ring finger on the fifth fret of the C string and pluck it.

Step 4: Next, place your index finger on the second fret of the C string.

Step 5: Finish the melody by playing the C string open.

The key is to practice this shift over and over until you get the hang of switching between strings. Try switching between other strings as well. We will look at one more exercise in basic tablature before learning chords which use tablature.

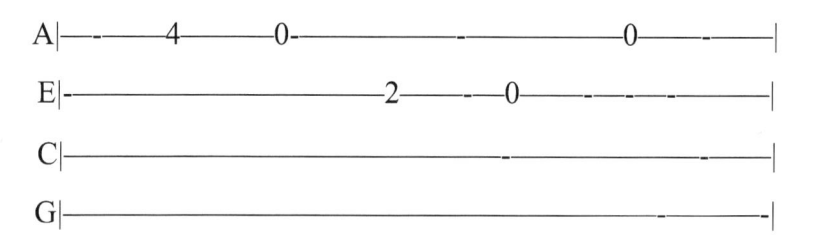

```
A|----4-----0---------------------0--------|
E|---------------2-----0-------------------|
C|----------------------------------------|
G|----------------------------------------|
```

The focus on the previous exercises was on the lower strings. Now we move to the higher strings. This exercise is admittedly more challenging but you can do it. Take it slowly at first and do not rush. Speed comes with time and practice. What is more important is that you play the melody accurately and read the tabs correctly.

Step 1: We start by playing the fourth fret of the A string. Use your ring finger.

Step 2: Then play the A string open.

Step 3: Place your index finger on the second fret of the E

string and then play it open.

Step 4: Finish the melody by playing the open A string.

Practice the melody and in your own time, speed up as much as you deem appropriate based on what sounds right to you. It might seem hard at first to group these notes together into a sequence but you'll get there as you improve with repetition.

Separate notes vs grouped notes

Another important element of reading tablature is when you see notes grouped together versus separate. Let's take a look at what this distinction entails.

Look at the two pieces of tablature on the following page. Can you spot the difference?

Diagram (a)

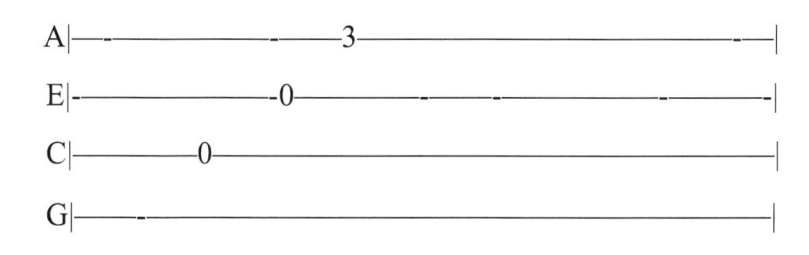

```
A|---            ------3-------                    --|
E|-            -0-          -       -        -   -|
C|         -0-                                      |
G|-- -                                              |
```

Diagram (b)

```
A|---   -3-                                      --|
E|-      -0-  -     -              -        -     |
C|      -0-                                        |
G|              - - -    -                         |
```

Both diagrams involve the same group of notes: the open C and E strings with the third fret of the A string. However, there is indeed a vital difference between these two diagrams. This is the spacing. When notes are separated as demonstrated in *diagram (a)*, the notes are meant to be played individually and not strummed as a chord. In other words, each note should be picked separately. In this case, you would start by playing the C string, then the E string and finishing on the A string respectively.

In the case of *diagram (b)*, the notes are in line with each other which we call a chord. The notes are meant to be strummed in unison. So instead of playing each note separately, you would have your index or middle finger on the third fret of the A string before playing any note. Then, you would strum the C, E and A strings together. We will come onto chords very shortly but keep in mind the difference between a sequence of notes and grouped notes. One little exercise you can try out is play *diagram (a)* and *(b)* one after the other. Familiarising yourself with the feel of different methods of ukulele playing in the initial stages is the difference between accelerating quickly and learning slower than you could otherwise learn.

One more example to illustrate this point would be as follows:

Diagram (c)

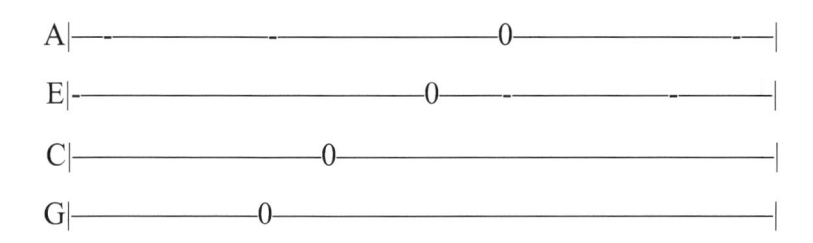

```
A|----------------------------0-----------|
E|-----------------------0----------------|
C|-----------------0----------------------|
G|------------0---------------------------|
```

Diagram (d)

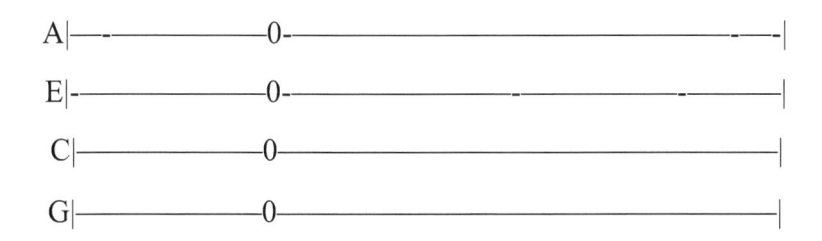

```
A|------------0---------------------------|
E|------------0---------------------------|
C|------------0---------------------------|
G|------------0---------------------------|
```

As we observed in the first two diagrams, diagram (c) is the individual notation and diagram (d) represents the grouped notes. This example is a mile simpler however as it is all open notes. Diagram (c) asks of us only to play through each note one by one whereas diagram (d) demands us to strum every string together and open. Hopefully this is simple enough.

Now it's time to look at chords.

Chords

Chords are groups of notes (typically between *2* and *5* notes) strummed in unison. In this chapter, you will be introduced to basic chord shapes and then you will learn how to play them together to form what are called **chord progressions**.

Chords are a step up from individual tabs since multiple notes are being played in one single strum plus there is the added expense of having to pick correctly and then change shape.

Do not fret! (n*o pun intended*) This chapter will help you with all of the potential hurdles and before you know it, you'll be jamming away through songs with ease. Be patient, practice each exercise and take your time. Learning chords on ukulele can be a frustrating process but keep with it. It is worth the hard work that you put in.

We'll be looking at the following chords to start off with :

C major, G major, A minor and F major.

We will begin with the chord that all beginners ought to know like the back of their hand. The *C major* chord.

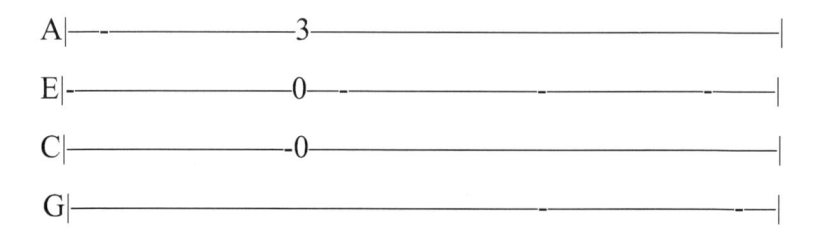

```
A|---            -3-                              |
E|-              -0---                      -   --|
C|               -0-                            --|
G|                                           -  --|
```

This is what the chord looks like when written out. C major on the ukulele is the simplest chord to play since it only involves one finger being used.

Step 1: To start the chord, place your index finger (pointer) on the third fret of the A string.

Step 2: Strum the C, E and A strings. i.e. the top three strings of the ukulele.

If you got it right, you should hear the beautiful sound of a C chord.

Do not move on to the next chord until you have a good grasp of the C chord. An exercise which you must learn to do is to play a new chord and then remove all your fingers from the instrument. After a few seconds, try to re-find the fingering and play the chord again from memory. This method, employed by top musicians (particularly guitarists) helps your muscle memory increase drastically. It is arduous at first but the more you try it, the better you'll get the hang of it.

Our second chord is the **G major** chord.

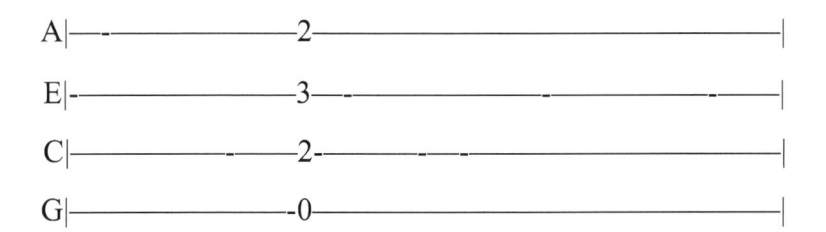

```
A|---------------2---------------------------------|
E|--------------3---- --              --  -----|
C|---------  ---2-- ---------   --            -----|
G|--------------  -0-------------------------------|
```

So right off the bat, I'm going to be completely honest with you: on every stringed instrument whether it be the mandolin, guitar or ukulele, the G chord has a way of somehow being the most frustrating chord to learn. Unfortunately, we have to roll with it and just face it head on. Again, once you learn the fingering for the chord, repeat the shape as hard as it may be. Muscle memory never fails a ukulele player!

Step 1: Place your index finger on the second fret of the C string.

Step 2: Place your ring finger (yes I know it feels weird) on the third fret of the E string.

Step 3: Finish with the middle finger tucked underneath it on the A string.

If you ever saw the 90s sitcom **Friends**, this is the chord shape that Phoebe called the 'bear claw' because your fingers resemble those of a creature with scrunched paws. Or maybe even Yoda from Star Wars…

Exercise

Before moving on to the third chord, it is time for an exercise. We have covered two essential chords and it would benefit you to focus on these before moving on. To really make these chords stick in your memory, you need to put them into practical use. So we are going to practice an exercise whereby you will play the C chord and the G chord in sequence as follows.

C　　　　　*G*　　　　　*C*　　　　　*G*

Take your time with it ! Practice it until it flows naturally and then move on to the next chord shape. It's important to practice every chord as you go along as opposed to cramming them in later. The more you become used to associating a chord name with its shape, the easier you'll find practicing songs later on when you have no visual prompter or tab to help you.

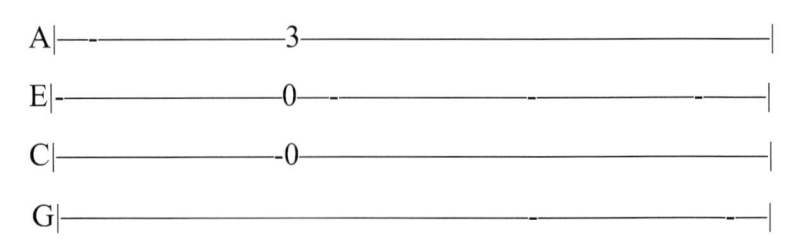

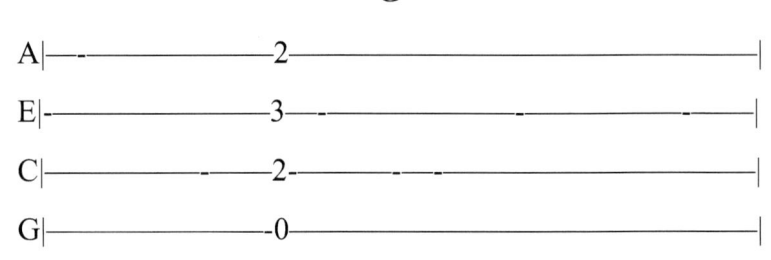

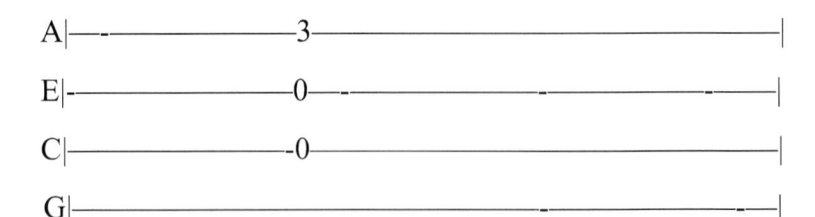

C

```
A|---————————3————————————————————|
E|-—————————0——-—————————-————————|
C|—————————-0—————————————————————|
G|———————————————————————————-————|
```

G

```
A|---————————2————————————————————|
E|-—————————3——-—————————-————————|
C|————————-2-—————————-———————————|
G|—————————-0—————————————————————|
```

C

```
A|---————————3————————————————————|
E|-—————————0——-—————————-————————|
C|—————————-0—————————————————————|
G|———————————————————————————-————|
```

G

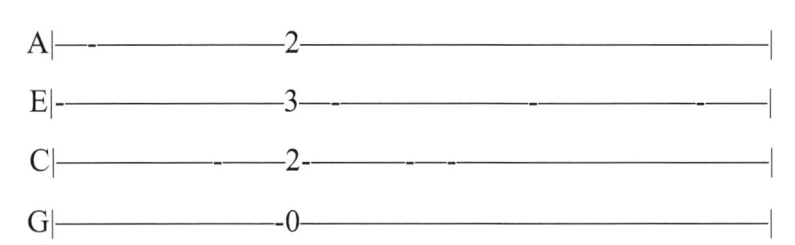

```
A|----------------2-------------------------|
E|--------------3---- -          -  --------|
C|------ -----2-          -  -              |
G|-----------0------------------------------|
```

Our third chord shape is A minor. This is similar to the C chord in that it involves a singe finger on the fretting hand.

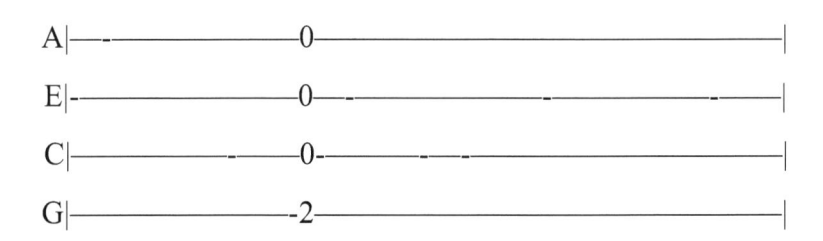

```
A|---- -----------0-------------------------|
E|--------------0---- -          -  --------|
C|------ -----0-          -  -              |
G|-----------2------------------------------|
```

Step 1: To play this chord, begin by placing your index finger or middle finger (if you prefer) in the second fret of the G string.

Step 2: That's pretty much it. Now you strum the four strings.

If you are new to music, minor chords are supposed to sound sad and they act really well with major chords (the 'happy' sounding chords). In modern pop music, you typically find one minor chord in a progression of four chords but we will come onto chord progressions in due course.

Exercise

It is time for an exercise again. At this point, having learned three chords: one of which was a pretty challenging one, we need to practice bringing them together and incorporating the A minor with the two major chords.

For this exercise, we are going to play a chord progression. It is simpler than it looks so give it as much of a chance as you can. Play it slowly and take as much time as you need to switch chord shapes.

The progression is:

C   G   Am   C

In this sequence, we are starting out on a C major chord, moving to G, then the A minor (which is arguably the most uphill part of this exercise) and then back to C. It's a challenge because shifting from a three finger chord to a one finger chord can be quite an experience when starting out. This exercise is not random nor pointless though because practicing it and getting a grasp of it will help you with three key aspects of ukulele playing.

1. Switching between chords.
2. Muscle memory and increased finger agility.
3. Returning back to the key note (C) after having played other chords.

Point three is particularly indispensable because in any genre of music, it is one thing to be able to switch chords but what makes a musician particularly skilled is the ability to return to the starting chord/note having gone through the progression. In this case, C major is your anchor. Focus on points 1 and 2 but also put extra practice into going from the G major and A minor back to the C major.

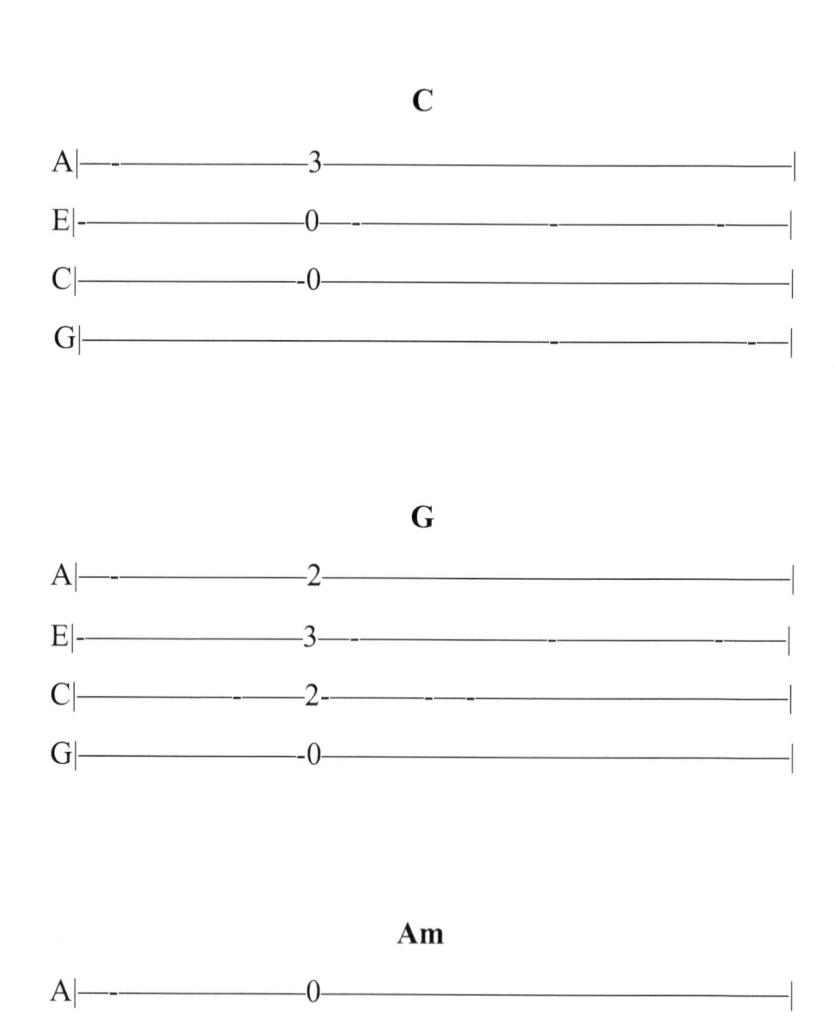

```
              C
A|------------3-------------------|
E|------------0-------------------|
C|------------0-------------------|
G|--------------------------------|
```

```
              G
A|------------2-------------------|
E|------------3-------------------|
C|------------2-------------------|
G|------------0-------------------|
```

```
              Am
A|------------0-------------------|
E|------------0-------------------|
C|------------0-------------------|
G|------------2-------------------|
```

C

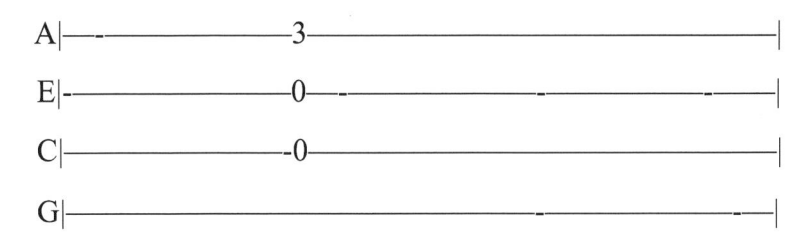

```
A|------3----------------------|
E|------0----------------------|
C|------0----------------------|
G|-----------------------------|
```

The next chord we will look at is the F major chord.

This chord can appear to be quite tricky but if you nail this one down, you'll really be making progress in your ukulele journey. The F major chord uses two fingers in what is actually quite a stretch if you're brand new. Don't panic though because you will get there. As repetitive as I have been about it: practice will make you the best uke player you can be.

```
A|------0----------------------|
E|------1----------------------|
C|------0----------------------|
G|------2----------------------|
```

The F chord is different to the previous chords we have looked at because the leading finger which for a lot of chords is typically the index finger, is actually the middle finger.

Step 1: Start by placing your middle finger on the second fret of the G string.

Step 2: Keeping the G string firmly pressed down, place your index finger on the first fret of the E string. Remember, we are skipping a string so be sure you aren't placing your index finger on the first fret of the C string otherwise you will get an A major chord which is fine but NOT what we are going for here.

If you're starting out, do not be disheartened if you find this fingering particularly difficult. You aren't expected to perfect the F major chord when you're just a few days into playing. However, in your own time and without rushing, do try to memorise the shape of the F chord. Another good exercise is performing the shape away from the instrument and just in your day to day life. The muscles in your hand will strengthen and become used to the stretch.

The final chord which we will look at is the D major chord. I wish I had better news for you but this chord is another tough one. Still, you need to be introduced to these chords because while they can be hard, they are essential and the D major chord is one of the most recurring chords in music.

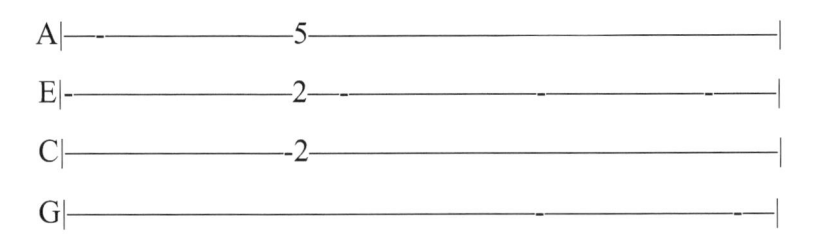

```
A|---------------5-------------------------------|
E|-------------2---------------------------------|
C|-------------2---------------------------------|
G|----------------------------------------------|
```

The D major is a three finger chord.

Step 1: Place your index finger on the second fret of the C string.

Step 2: Place your middle finger just underneath it on the second fret of the E string.

Step 3: Now for the stretch. Place your pinky finger (*yes that's right: pinky finger*) on the fifth fret of the A string. Strum the chord.

You might be aware that the chord looks a bit peculiar. It's probably because you are leaving a two fret gap. Don't worry, it's meant to feel and look like that. Strum the entire chord making sure your index and middle finger are not muting each other. If your fingers are muting these strings a bit, it's because your shape needs to be more accurate.

Accurate fingerings are what make the ukulele sound crisp and professional. If you do find yourself in a situation of buzzing or muting, bend the fingers a little bit and make sure you are pressing hard enough on the string. There will be a little bit of pain if you are new to stringed fretted instruments but your finger tips will callus with time and practice and no longer cause any issues.

We have now covered the basic chords needed when starting out on the ukulele. There are many other chords which you need to learn and they are included on the opening page so please do refer to the diagram and learn some of the other chords at your own volition. I would recommend looking at the A major chord and B minor chord to begin with.

A major

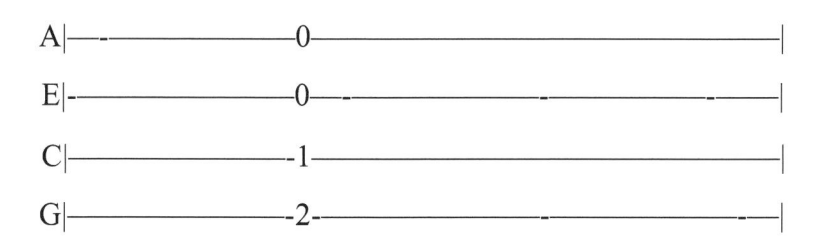

```
A|---------------0-------------------------|
E|--------------0------------------- -----|
C|---------------1-------------------------|
G|---------------2------------------- ----|
```

B minor

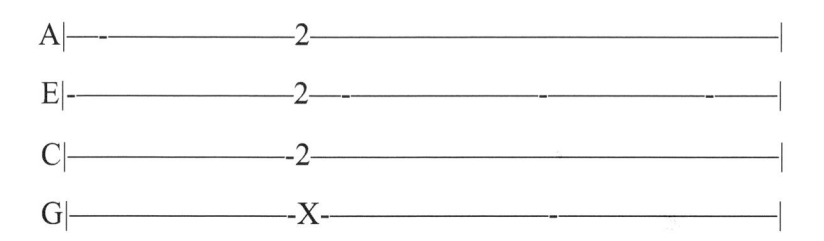

```
A|---------------2-------------------------|
E|--------------2------------------- -----|
C|---------------2-------------------------|
G|---------------X------------------- -----|
```

In the B minor chord, you might be wondering what the X is. In tablature, when you see an X, it signifies that you do not play that string at all.

With what's been covered so far, you should have all the knowledge and skill required to teach yourself some of the other chord shapes so don't be shy or intimidated, you can do it and I believe you will be an awesome ukulele player who is going to be able to play any chord on demand in no time!

Chord Progressions

Chord progressions put the chords you've learned into practice and turn sound into music. We have already looked at a few with the C, G and A minor chords.

Here are a few for you to try out:

1. C   F   C   G   C

2. C   G   Am   F

3. D   G   G   D

4. Am   F   C   G   C

5. F   G   F   G   C

6. C   Am   G   Am   C

7. C   D   C   G   C

8. C   C   F   Am   C

Strumming

When first starting out on the ukulele or any stringed instrument for that matter, it is tempting to just strum downwards. However, the earlier you learn how to strum properly, the quicker you'll pick it up. Ukulele players determine how to strum their instrument based on strumming patterns. That is, when the strum downwards and upwards in different amounts. For example, a typical strum is:

down down up

(D D U)

This means that the player, with their right hand, will strum down twice and back up once. Strumming down means starting at the bottom string (G) and moving down while hitting all four strings and letting them ring out at once. Strumming upwards involves starting with the high string (A) and doing the same thing as down-strumming but in reverse.

Songs rarely start with an up-strum and typically begin with a down-strum. You can practice strumming slowly and build it up to a normal speed. This is an effective way to practice. Don't feel discouraged if you don't get it at first.

It does take time to perfect it and soon, you'll be able to strum to all sorts of strumming patterns. Here are three common strumming patterns that you will come across.

(I recommend that you start practicing these patterns on one chord first before playing multiple chords. Once you feel you've got the hang of it, try two chords and then three or four. After, you may apply strumming patterns to the previous exercises).

D. D. U. D. U. D

(x4)

D. U. D. U. D. U. D. U

(x4)

D. U. D. D. U

(x4)

(PRACTICE SPACE)

n.b. these next three pages have been designed for you to write out your own tablature based on what you've learned so far. You might use this page to create your own chord progressions or maybe a melody. You are encouraged to use this space however you see fit as such an exercise will help your creative abilities.

```
A|------------------------------------------------|
E|------------------------------------------------|
C|------------------------------------------------|
G|------------------------------------------------|


A|------------------------------------------------|
E|------------------------------------------------|
C|------------------------------------------------|
G|------------------------------------------------|


A|------------------------------------------------|
E|------------------------------------------------|
C|------------------------------------------------|
G|------------------------------------------------|
```

```
A|--------------------------------------------------|
E|--------------------------------------------------|
C|--------------------------------------------------|
G|--------------------------------------------------|


A|--------------------------------------------------|
E|--------------------------------------------------|
C|--------------------------------------------------|
G|--------------------------------------------------|


A|--------------------------------------------------|
E|--------------------------------------------------|
C|--------------------------------------------------|
G|--------------------------------------------------|


A|--------------------------------------------------|
E|--------------------------------------------------|
C|--------------------------------------------------|
G|--------------------------------------------------|
```

```
A|--------------------------------------------------|
E|--------------------------------------------------|
C|--------------------------------------------------|
G|--------------------------------------------------|


A|--------------------------------------------------|
E|--------------------------------------------------|
C|--------------------------------------------------|
G|--------------------------------------------------|


A|--------------------------------------------------|
E|--------------------------------------------------|
C|--------------------------------------------------|
G|--------------------------------------------------|


A|--------------------------------------------------|
E|--------------------------------------------------|
C|--------------------------------------------------|
G|--------------------------------------------------|
```

Technique 1: Pull-Offs & Hammer-ons

In the previous chapters, we covered the essential basics of the ukulele. Now we move on to techniques which are designed to help you perfect and improve your playing. A technique in some ways might appear easier than a whole new concept on ukulele but in other ways, techniques are actually harder. Not because they take more skill but because they help a player understand the music they are playing as opposed to just following along with tabs and sheet music. To a large extent, they are the difference between a player who can simply play a few notes and a musician who knows the purpose of those notes.

What is meant by **purpose**?

Sometimes, especially in basic ukulele, you might play a set of notes which make up a melody. However, knowing why you are playing those notes and how they fit in with the song is a whole other thing. Techniques such as the ones we will cover in the following chapters help you understand the music you are playing. In this way, with confidence and practice, you'll be able to make any melody your own.

We start with pull-offs and hammer-ons.

Both are remarkably common in the world of electric guitar and even bass. Advanced ukulele players use them all of the time too and while they sound like complicated or weird concepts, they really aren't if you learn how to practice them properly and you get the technique right.

1. What is a *hammer-on*?

While the name sounds like something out of nordic war epic, the name actually makes complete sense with what it is. A hammer-on is when you play a note and then play a different note on the same string but instead of picking it you just hit it with a different finger i.e. hammering on. Your finger acts as a 'hammer' of sorts to strike a note without plucking it, using the momentum from the previously strum note.

In ukulele tablature, a hammer-on is identified by this symbol:

‘

Let's take a look at how a hammer-on might look like in a piece of music.

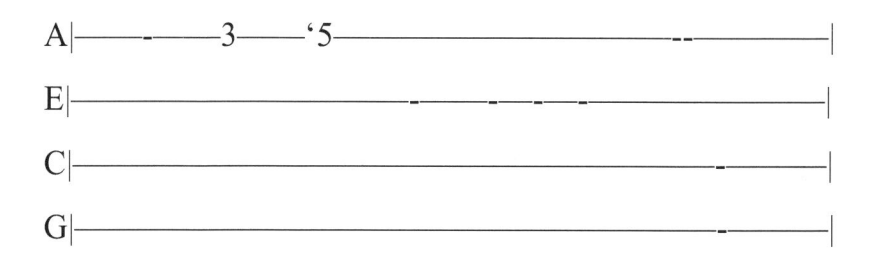

```
A|------3----'5----------------------|
E|----------------------------------|
C|----------------------------------|
G|----------------------------------|
```

In this example, we are going from the third fret of the A string to the fifth fret. So what's so unique about this? Simply, instead of picking the fifth fret as an individual note, you don't. Let me break it down for you step by step so you can fully understand how this technique works.

Step 1: Place your index finger on the third fret of the A string. Pluck it or pick it as you normally would.

Step 2: With some force, hit the fifth fret of the A string with your ring finger without plucking or picking it separately. If done right, you would have heard the fifth fret being played without using your right hand. This is a hammer-on.

The function of hammer-ons might seem banal and useless in the context of an exercise but when you use them in songs, they not only improve the quality of your skill-set but they can make a lick or riff sounds very professional.

Before we move on, let's try out an exercise where hammer-ons are used. The exercise is straight forward but make sure to play it slowly at first getting the hang of the fingering. When you're confident enough to do so, speed it up at your own volition.

Exercise:

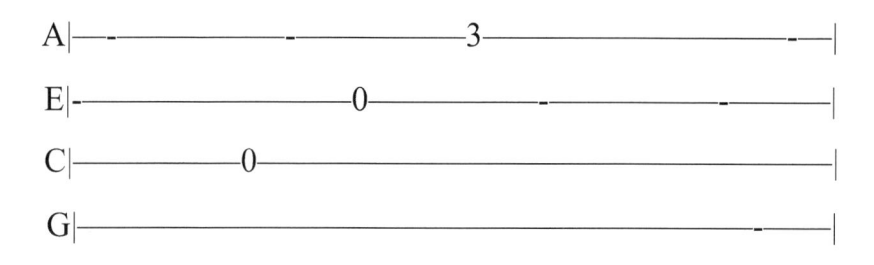

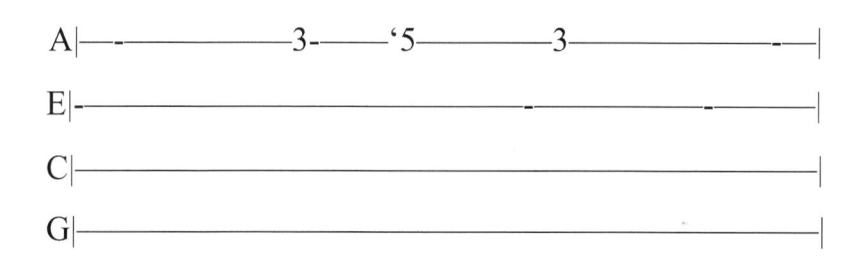

```
A|--                    -        -3-                    -|
E|-                      -0-                  -        - |
C|           -0-                                         |
G|                                              -        |
```

```
A|--           -3-     '5-         -3-              -|
E|-                              -              -     |
C|                                                    |
G|                                                    |
```

Let's see what's going on here.

Step 1: Begin by playing the open C and E strings.

Step 2: Now, place your index finger on the third fret of the A string as you did in the first exercise.

Step 3: Now for the hammer-on. Hit the fifth fret using just your ring finger.

Step 4: Go back to the third fret of the A string with your index finger and pick it normally.

2. What is a *pull-off*?

A pull off is almost the opposite of a hammer-on, but not quite. A pull-off is what it sounds like. It is when you go down a note by 'pulling' off from a note. Instead of removing your finger entirely and playing the next note separately, you will use the finger already on the fret by push it down, letting go and letting the string ring out. Let's use the same example as we did with the hammer-on.

In ukulele tablature, a pull-off is identified by this symbol:

//

```
A|--------5//------3-------------------------------|
E|------------------------------------------------|
C|------------------------------------------------|
G|------------------------------------------------|
```

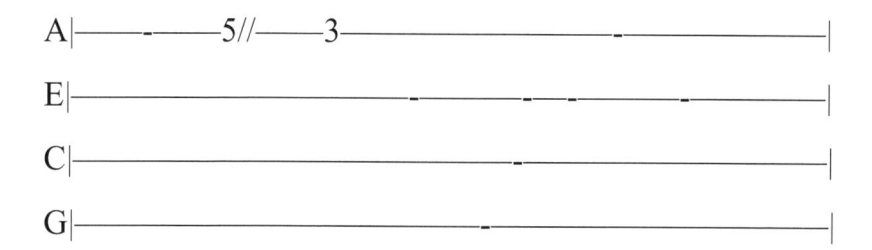

Following on from the last example, let's say you have played the fifth fret of the A string and want to go down to the third fret. Instead of playing it as a lone note (by re-picking the string on the third fret), you want to perform a pull-off to make the sequence smoother.

Step 1: Place your ring finger on the fifth fret of the A string.

Step 2: While you are playing the fifth fret, have your index finger already on the third fret ready to be played. So now, you should have two fingers on the A string: one on the third fret and one on the fifth.

Step 3: Pick the fifth fret as you normally would.

Step 4: Now quickly, as the note is playing, pull the string downwards with your fretting finger and finally off the string while letting it ring out. This should let the third fret of the A string (the C note) ring out. This is a pull-off as you are literally pulling off from a note onto one lower than it.

Technique 2: Soloing in C

With many students who are only a few lessons into playing the ukulele, all things to do with C major are very appealing. It's always the first chord people learn and it is usually the go-to key for beginners who try to learn songs on their own? Why is this? Simply because it is easy. It's a one finger chord using one note on one fret. Plus, many pop songs use C as the basis.

So knowing that C is popular, beautiful sounding and straight forward, we've decided to dedicate a chapter to making your C chord go further. That is, how can you as a debutant on ukulele make the C chord become something more. Specifically, we will look at how notes in the C major scale on the ukulele can help you write easy but cool sounding solos using minimal effort and a solid understanding of the notes in C.

Diagram (a)

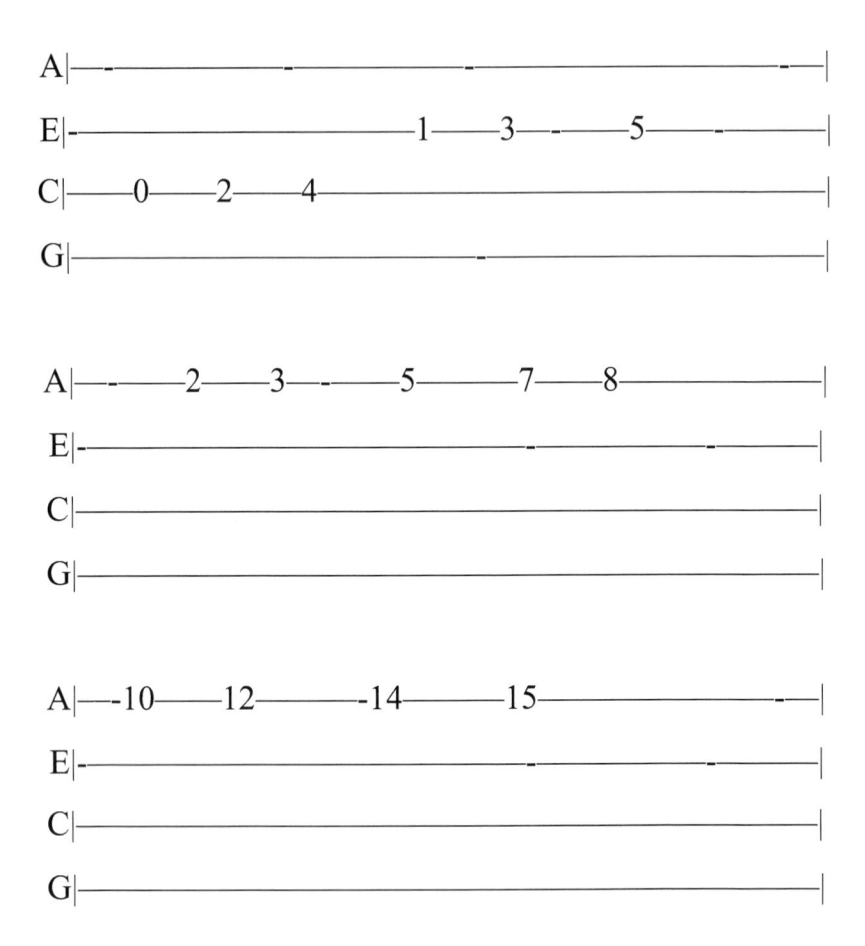

```
A|---                 -              -          -|
E|-                  -1--3---5-         -|
C|--0--2--4                                      |
G|-                          -                    |

A|---2--3---5--7--8-                             |
E|-                      -       -              -|
C|-                                              |
G|-                                              |

A|--10--12----14----15-              -|
E|-                      -       -              -|
C|-                                              |
G|-                                              |
```

Take a look at the diagram above. This diagram is not a melody but rather a the C major scale. They are all notes which can be formulated (however you please) to make a melody in C. In fact, the traditional song "Amazing Grace" which is in C major uses these notes.

We'll take a look at the song shortly, but first, I want you to play the scale about and familiarise yourself with the individual notes. The next step once you are up to speed with the C major scale is putting it into practice. We'll start with two basic compositions in C major that we have put together. Then, you will be encouraged to create your own using the notes from the C major scale as demonstrated in diagram (a).

Composition 1:

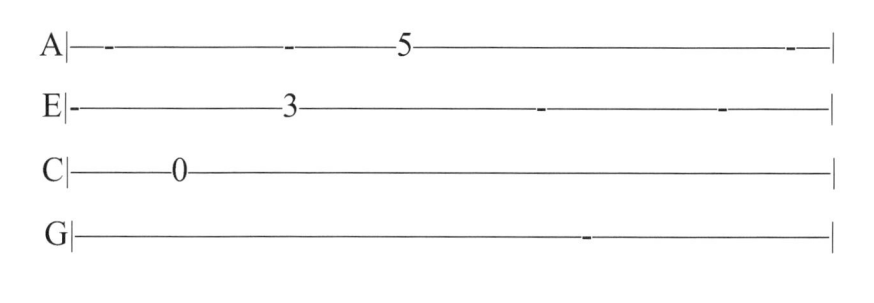

```
A|----------------------5----------------------|
E|-----------3---------------------------------|
C|------0--------------------------------------|
G|---------------------------------------------|
```

```
A|----7---------5---------8---------7----------|
E|---------------------------------------------|
C|---------------------------------------------|
G|---------------------------------------------|
```

```
A|-----------------------------------------------------  -----|
E|-----------------------------------------  ----------  -----|
C|--------2--------0----------0-------------------  ----------|
G|------------------------------------------------------------|




A|-----------------------------  -----------------------  ----|
E|--------3-----1---------------------  ---------------  -----|
C|---------------------------4--------4-----------------------|
G|------------------------------------------------------------|
```

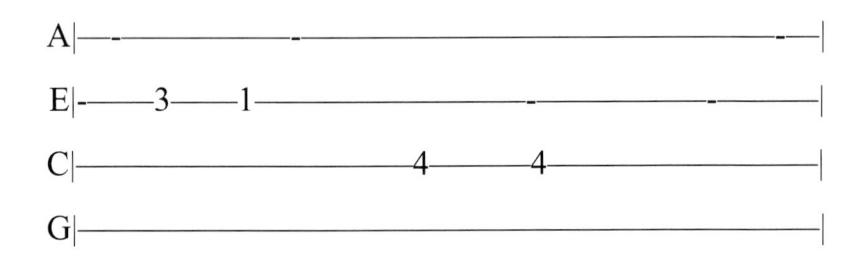

Composition 2:

```
A|------------------------------------------|
E|----0------3------0------5----------------|
C|------------------------------------------|
G|------------------------------------------|


A|----5------7----0------3------2-----------|
E|------------------------------------------|
C|------------------------------------------|
G|------------------------------------------|


A|--------------------------3---------------|
E|------------3-----------------------------|
C|------------------------------------------|
G|------------------------------------------|


A|---------------------3--------------------|
E|-----------------0------------------------|
C|--------------0---------------------------|
G|------------------------------------------|
```

It is now your turn to write out a composition in C using the C major scale and the examples in the previous two compositions.

```
A|---- -                                              -|
E|-                              -                 -  |
C|-                                                   |
G|-                                                   |
```

```
A|---- -                                             -|
E|-                                     -          -  |
C|-                                                   |
G|-                                                   |
```

```
A|---- -                                    -         |
E|-                                   -           -   |
C|-                                                   |
G|-                                                   |
```

```
A|----   -                                              -  |
E|-                              -                 -       |
C|                                                         |
G|                                                         |


A|---       -                                           -  |
E|-                        -                 -            |
C|                                                         |
G|                                                         |


A|---       -                                        -  -  |
E|-                                 -             -        |
C|                                                         |
G|                                                         |


A|---       -                                              -  |
E|-                                    -          -           |
C|                                                            |
G|                                                            |
```

Practice is everything when it comes to playing the ukulele and so to hit home the point of soloing in C major, it's time for a practice song.§ Play it slowly and take your time. As aforementioned, the following tune is in the key of C and uses many of the techniques and concepts that have been covered in the book so far.

PRACTICE SONG

Amazing Grace

```
A|---------------3---------------|
E|----3--------------------------|
C|--------------0----------------|
G|-------------------------------|
```

```
A|-----7--5--3--5--7-------------|
E|-------------------------------|
C|-------------------------------|
G|-------------------------------|
```

```
A|-------5------3----------------|
E|-------------------------------|
C|-------------------------------|
G|-------------------------------|
```

```
A|----------------------------------|
E|-----5---------3------------------|
C|---------------0------------------|
G|----------------------------------|
```

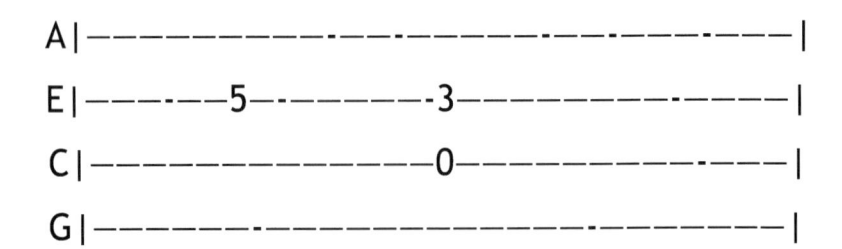

```
A|------3----7--5----3--------------|
E|--3-------------------------------|
C|----------------------------------|
G|----------------------------------|
```

```
A|----5------7----5-----------------|
E|----------------------------------|
C|----------------------------------|
G|----------------------------------|
```

```
A|----10----------------------------|
E|----------------------------------|
C|----------------------------------|
G|----0-----------------------------|
```

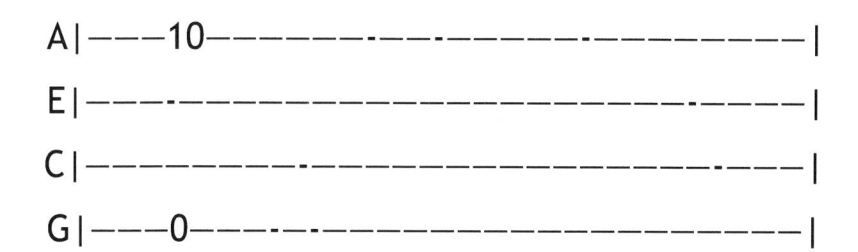

```
A|-----7-----10-----10--------------|
E|----------------------------------|
C|-----------------0----------------|
G|----------------------------------|
```

```
A|-----7----5-----3-----5----7------|
E|----------------------------------|
C|----------------------------------|
G|----------------------------------|
```

```
A|————5————3———————————————|
E|————————————————3——5——3————————|
C|——————————————————————————————|
G|——————————————————————————————|
```

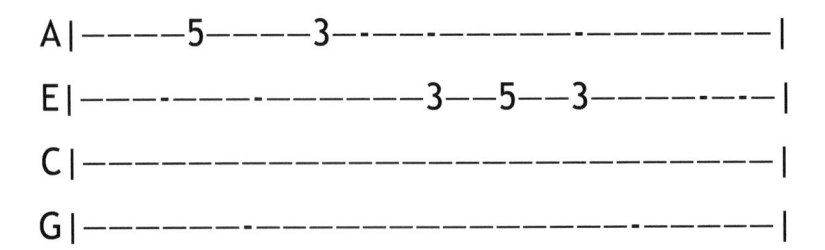

```
A|——————————3——7————————————————|
E|———3——————————————————————————|
C|——————————————————————————————|
G|——————————————————————————————|
```

```
A|————————5————3—————5——————————|
E|——————————————————————————————|
C|——————————————————————————————|
G|——————————————————————————————|
```

```
A|————————3—·——-3—·—·————————|
E|————·———·————————————·——|
C|————————————————————·———|
G|——————·—————————————————|




A|——————————·——·————·———————|
E|————·———3—·———————————·———|
C|———————————————0——————————|
G|——————·———————————————————|




A|—————————·———3-——————————|
E|————-3————·————————·————|
C|———————————-0—————————·——|
G|———————·—————————————————|
```

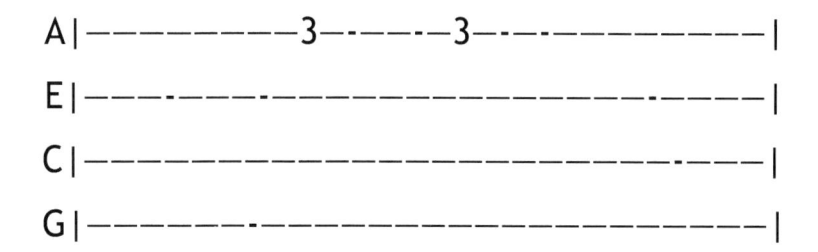

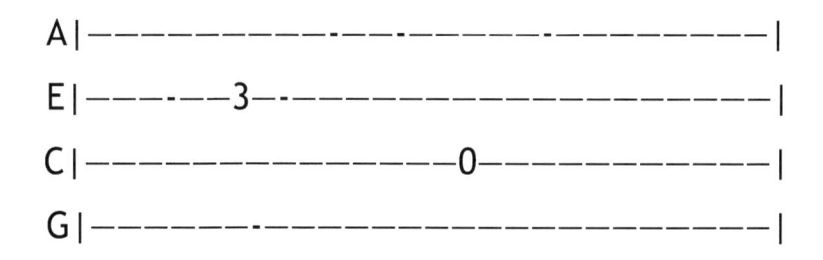

```
A|-----7--5--3--5--7-----------|
E|-----------------------------|
C|-----------------------------|
G|-----------------------------|
```

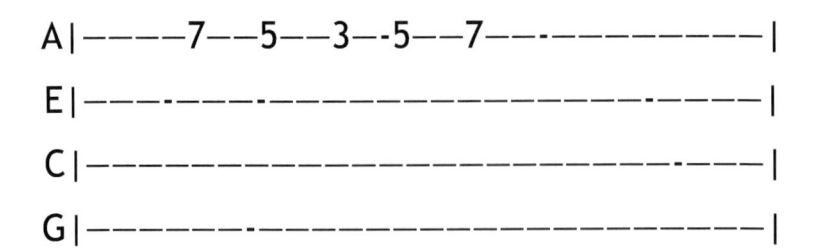

```
A|-------5-----3---------------|
E|-----------------------------|
C|-----------------------------|
G|-----------------------------|
```

```
A|-----------------------------|
E|-----5---------3-------------|
C|---------------0-------------|
G|-----------------------------|
```

```
A|------3----7---5--.--3----------|
E|--3--.--------------------------|
C|-----------------------------.--|
G|--------------------------------|
```

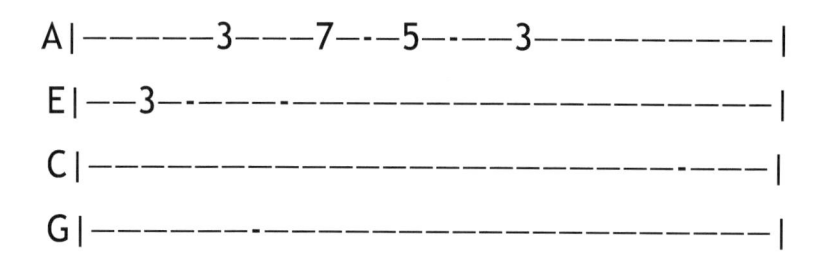

```
A|----5------7.---.-5---.---------|
E|---.----------------------.-----|
C|-----------------------------.--|
G|--------.-----------------------|
```

```
A|---10-----------.----------.----|
E|----.----------------------.----|
C|----------------.-------------.-|
G|---0--------.-------------------|
```

```
A|-----7-----10-----10------------|
E|--------------------------------|
C|-----------------0--------------|
G|--------------------------------|
```

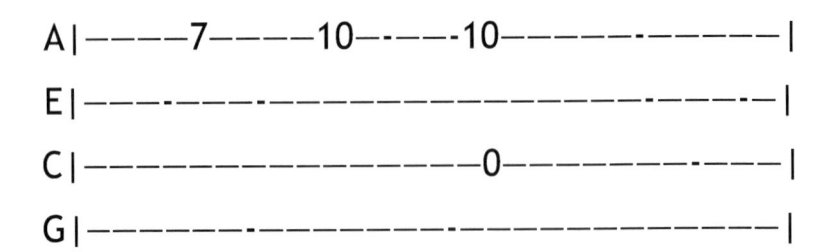

```
A|-----7----5-----3-----5-----7------|
E|-----------------------------------|
C|-----------------------------------|
G|-----------------------------------|
```

```
A|-----5-----3-----------------------|
E|-----------------3----5----3-------|
C|-----------------------------------|
G|-----------------------------------|
```

```
A|--------3--7---------------|
E|---3----------------------|
C|--------------------------|
G|--------------------------|
```

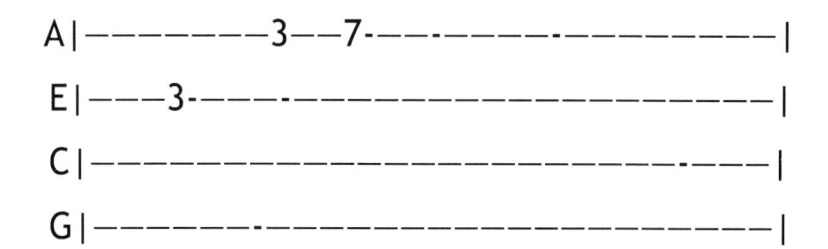

```
A|--------5-----3-----5------|
E|--------------------------|
C|--------------------------|
G|--------------------------|
```

```
A|--------3-----3------------|
E|--------------------------|
C|--------------------------|
G|--------------------------|
```

```
A|------------------------|
E|-----3------------------|
C|--------------0---------|
G|------------------------|
```

Technique 3: Barring

In this chapter, you will be introduced to the concept of barring. This is for all intent and purposes a more advanced technique. If you have had any experience playing the guitar, at some point you would have come across barre chords. Whenever students are taught them for the first time, there is always an unanimous moan because barre chords by nature are not easy for the budding beginner. Well, there's more bad news for you: if you're learning the uke to get away from such a technique, you're in for a long night because lo and behold, barre chords exist on ukulele too!

If you have not played guitar before, don't worry. Everything will be explained in this chapter. Let's get into what barre chords are.

I want you cast your mind back to when we learned the D major chord.

It looks like this:

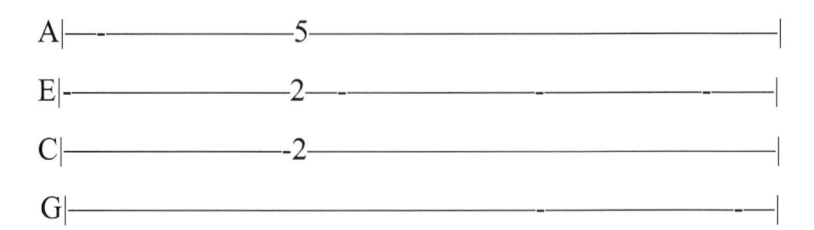

```
A|---------------5-----------------------------|
E|-------------2---- -                    -    |
C|--------------2------------------------------|
G|---------------------------------------    --|
```

At least, that's the way you were taught in the introduction to chords. Now that you've become more acquainted with your instrument, it's time for me to drop a bomb shell: there is a more professional and detailed version of a D chord.

It looks like this:

```
A|---------------5-----------------------------|
E|-------------2---- -                    -    |
C|--------------2------------------------------|
G|-------------2-------------------------    --|
```

The big deal is : how are you supposed to play the G string on the second fret when your index finger, middle finger and ring finger are all occupied? You might say that we can use our pinky and adjust our hand but this is illogical and would make playing the chord exceedingly uncomfortable for our fingers.

So we do what is called ***barring***.

Barring means that instead of using multiple fingers on the same fret (in this case, the second fret), we use one finger (usually our index finger) to cover multiple strings on the same fret. Therefore, we would barre the second fret with our index finger. How is this done, you might ask? Let's take it step by step, as always.

Step 1: Take your index finger and press it hard against the second fret covering all the strings. It will look a bit strange but it's meant to. Ensure your finger is covering every string and is firmly pressing down the fret. This is the trickiest step and it's common to not press hard enough. Don't give up if it seems hard at first.

Step 2: Use your pinky to play the fifth fret of the A string.

Step 3: Strum the chord. If this is your first time barring, it is not unusual for some of the strings to sound muted or blocked. In this instance, press harder with your index finger. I'm afraid there is no easier way around this and it's something you need to persevere with until it clicks. Try not to get frustrated and please ensure you don't injure yourself in the process. It's always better to walk away from a technique for a while before returning to it later than causing yourself grief in the moment.

The shape of the barre chord which we have looked at can be used *anywhere* on the fretboard. Let's look at an E major chord which uses the same barring but instead of starting on the second fret, we have our root on the fourth fret.

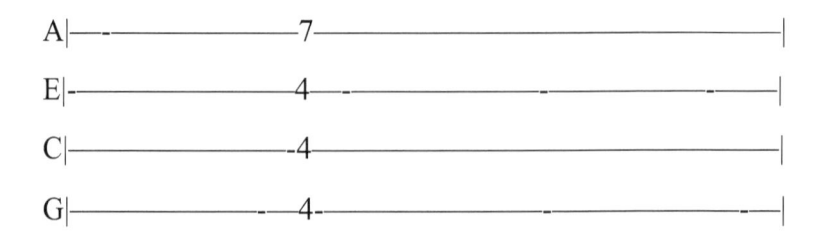

```
A|---------------7-------------------------------|
E|-------------4------- -            -        ---|
C|--------------4--------------------------------|
G|--------------4--                 -          --|
```

Try this one out for yourself!

Technique 4: Fifth & Seventh Chords

Fifth and seventh chords are used a lot in jazz music. On ukulele, you can incorporate them in just about any style of playing and they sound absolutely delightful. We start with seventh chords.

What are *seventh chords*?

A seventh chord is a regular chord with one key difference: it contains a note which is seven notes above the root note. So if we are playing an F major chord, we would include an E note because E is seven notes above the F.

F G A B C D E

Normally, the F major chord would contain:

F A C

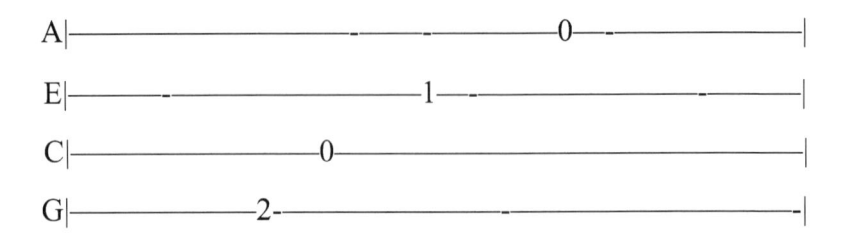

```
A|------------------------------0---------|
E|-----------------------1----------------|
C|-----------0----------------------------|
G|-----2----------------------------------|
```

In the diagram above, the second fret of the G string is an A note, the open C string is inevitably a C note, the first fret of the E string produces an F note and the open A string is also an A note. So a regular F major chord on the ukulele is composed of an F note, 2 A notes, and a C note. Simply put: F, A, and C.

So how do we transform it into a seventh? As aforementioned, we add an E note.

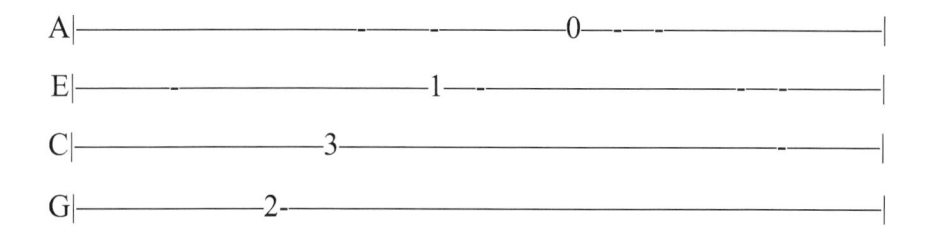

```
A|----------------------------------0---------------|
E|------------------------1-------------------------|
C|----------------3---------------------------------|
G|----------2---------------------------------------|
```

This is what it looks like. To achieve the F7 chord (the name of the F major chord when the seventh note is added):

Step 1: Place your middle finger on the second fret of the G string.

Step 2: Then, place your ring finger on the third fret of the C string. **This is the E note.**

Step 3: Finally, place your index finger on the first fret of the E string and strum the entire chord.

The best part of playing seventh chords is that you can incorporate them in any song. You can even turn regular songs into more jazzy sounding versions by adding one or two of them into your playing. Note that not every chord you play in a jazz song needs to be a seventh. Even one can change the dynamic. Try this chord pattern:

C G Am F7

We encountered C, G, and A minor in the previous chapter so if you need to familiarise yourself with these, go back for a recap if need be.

Let's look at another seventh chord. This one is the C major 7 or C7. Just like with the F7, we take the seventh note from the C and add it into our chord shape.

The seventh note of a C major is B.

<u>C</u> D E F G A <u>B</u>

Normally our C chord looks like this:

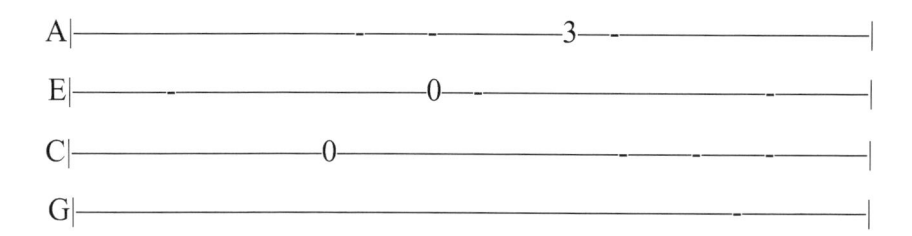

```
A|------------------------   -   -3---  -------------|
E|-------  -   -----------0---  -------------   -----|
C|--------------0------------------------   -  ------|
G|----------------------------------------------  ---|
```

It consists of G E and C. Luckily, on ukulele, adding a B note to the C chord is very easy.

Notice how there are two C notes in our C major chord: one on the third fret of the A string and one which is the open C string.

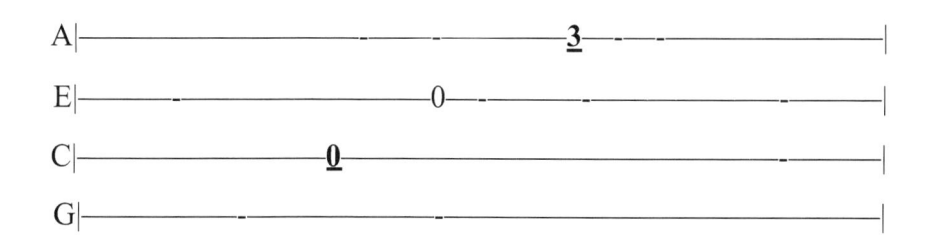

```
A|------------------------   -   -3---  -------------|
E|-------  -   -----------0---  -------------   -----|
C|--------------0------------------------   -  ------|
G|----------  -   --------  -----------------------  |
```

Since we already have a C note on the open C string, all we have to do is turn our C note on the A string into a B note. This is the second fret of the A string.

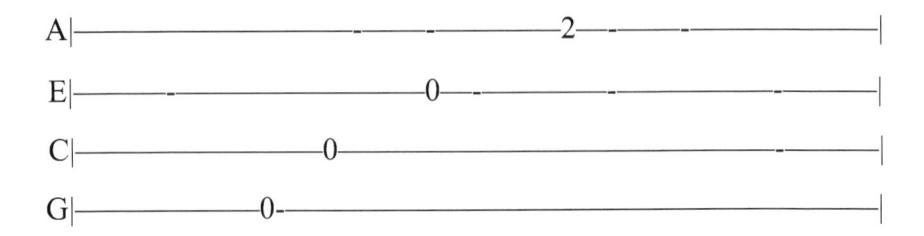

```
A|---------------------------2---------|
E|------------------0------------------|
C|---------0---------------------------|
G|----0--------------------------------|
```

This now makes a C7 chord because we now have a G, C, E and **B** note.

We have now had a look at two jazz chords. Let's put them together in a pattern:

C7 F7 G

Do not be intimidated by this chord progression. You have seen all of the above chords before. Putting them together takes practice but you will soon realise that it is much simpler than it appears.

We have covered the C7 and the F7 in this chapter. In the previous chapter, we looked at G major. Take your time and do not rush but at the same time, try to play them in the above order.

Before moving on to our second jazz technique, we will look at one final seventh chord. The G major 7 or G7 chord.

As with the C7 and F7, we first have to work out what the seventh note of the G major 7 is.

GABCDEF

It is the F note. Regularly, a G major chord contains a G, D and E:

```
A|-----------------2---------|
E|-----------4---------------|
C|--------2------------------|
G|------0--------------------|
```

When adding the seventh, this becomes G, D, E and F forming the G7 chord. One which is used often in jazz music.

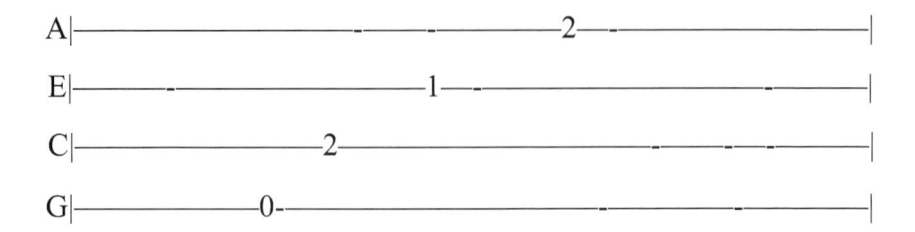

```
A|------------------------2----|
E|----------------1------------|
C|--------2--------------------|
G|----0------------------------|
```

Step 1: In order to achieve this chord, we start with the same form as the G major by playing the open G string and placing your middle finger on the second fret of the C string.

Step 2: Place your index (pointer) finger on the first fret of the E string. **This is the F note.**

Step 3: Finish by placing your ring finger on the second fret of the A string.

We have now covered the basics of the seventh chord and how you can achieve a magical jazz sound by simply rectifying basic chords by adding a seventh note. You can turn any chord into a seventh by simply adding that note into the equation. For guidance, here are the seventh notes you need for each chord you might play.

A: **A** B C D E F **G**

B: **B** C D E F G **A**

C: **C** D E F G A **B**

D: **D** E F G A B **C**

E: **E** F G A B C **D**

F: **F** G A B C D **E**

G: **G** A B C D E **F**

What is a *fifth chord*?

Fifth chords are also jazz chords. They give a warmer vibe than seventh chords and in this way, they complement seventh chords perfectly. Once you learn about fifth chords, you can mix and max them with seventh chords to create a beautiful jazz medley.

In the next lesson, we will focus specifically on how to form jazz chord progressions and how to put these chords together.

Much like the seventh chords, fifth chords work on the principle of numeracy. To find a fifth chord, you take the root note and count five notes above it. For the first example, we will be looking at an F5 chord, also known as the F major fifth chord.

As we learned in the previous lesson, the seventh of F is E.

<u>F</u> G A B C D <u>E</u>

The fifth on the other hand is C.

<u>F</u> G A B <u>C</u>

So in order to play the F5 chord, we need to add a C. Now you might be confused and say that F **already has** a C in it: **F A C** make up an F major chord.

However, this is where 5th chords are different to seventh chords.

While with seventh chords, the seventh note is added, in fifth chords, particularly in jazz, a fifth note takes priority over the root note and replaces it completely.

What does that mean? It means, you add the fifth note which in this case is C and we remove the F note entirely. In essence, the new note replaces the original note. So in the case of F5, we keep the A and C but use the extra C which is the fifth to take over the F note. It is still an F based chord but the F is what we call '*assumed*'.

In jazz music, assumed notes are not played but implied through the makeup of the other notes.

However, on ukulele, because we are limited to four strings, we do not eliminate the note completely as we normally would, but rather, we emphasise the fifth to almost silence the root note.

So an F5 looks like this.

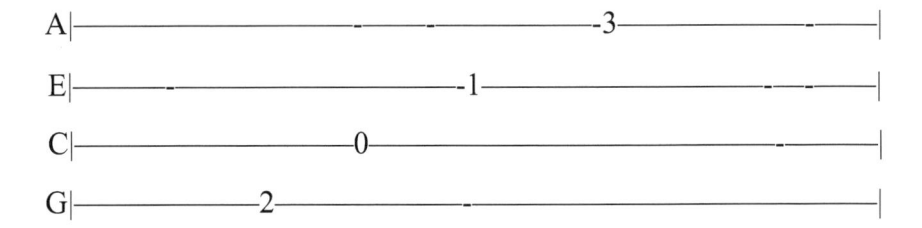

```
A|---------------------- - ---------3-----------------  -  ---|
E|---------- - ------------------1-------------------------  ---|
C|----------------------0------------------------------- - ---|
G|----------2----------------------- - ------------------------|
```

Let's break it down. We begin with the second fret of the G string which is the A note. Then we have the open C string. Next, we play the first fret of the E string and finally we end on that fifth note which takes priority. This is C and is played on the third fret of the A string.

Step 1: Place your middle finger on the second fret of the G string.

Step 2: Place your index finger on the first fret of the E string.

Step 3: Finish the chord by placing your ring finger on the third fret of the A string.

Strum the chord and listen to the beautiful warm jazz chord that has been created. At this point, give yourself a pat on the back as fifth chords are not easy and can be quite challenging to understand.

Now we'll take a look at a C5 chord. This is a welcome chord at this point because it is by far the simplest fifth chord that you will come across when playing jazz ukulele.

The fifth of C is G.

<u>C</u> D E F <u>G</u>

To play the C5 chord, our emphasis will be on the G note.

```
A|--------------------------  -  -3-----  -----------|
E|--------  -  -------------3-----------  --------  -|
C|-----------------0----------------------------  --|
G|----------0----------------  --------------------|
```

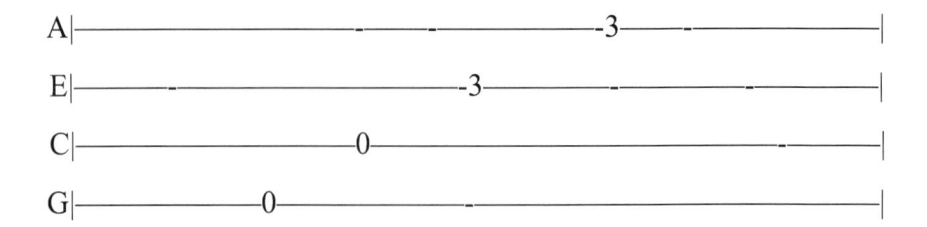

Step 1: Play the open G string and open C strings.

Step 2: Place your index finger on the third fret of the E string. This is our fifth (G note).

Step 3: Place your middle finger on the third fret of the A string.

Strum the chord.

It is worth noting that you can use whatever fingers you feel most comfortable using. The above is simply a recommendation.

The last fifth chord which we will explore is the G5, also known as the G major fifth chord.

The fifth of the G is D.

G A B C D

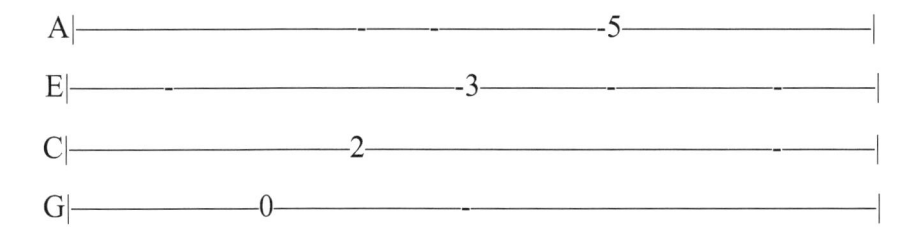

```
A|------------------------------5-----------------|
E|---------------------3--------------------------|
C|--------------2---------------------------------|
G|--------0---------------------------------------|
```

The G5 chord closely resembles the G major chord which we learned earlier in the book. The prime difference is that instead of playing the second fret of the A string which would be a **B** note, we play the fifth fret which is the D note. This completes our fifth chord.

To play the G5:

Step 1: Place your index finger on the second fret of the C string.

Step 2: Place your middle finger on the third fret of the E string. This might feel odd at first because you are essentially tucking your middle finger underneath your index finger but it'll become more natural as you practice the chord shape more regularly.

Step 3: Use your pinky to play the fifth fret of the A string. You can in theory use your ring finger but this will stretch the muscles in that finger in an uncomfortable manner.

Exercise:

It is now time to put your knowledge to good use and work on some chord progressions to get you started with writing your own pieces on ukulele using fifth and seventh chords. All of the chord progressions in this lesson are based on the chords covered in earlier chapters.

We will begin with the first progression:

C C C7 C7 F7 F7 C

This progression is in the key of C.

```
A|---------------------- - ----------3------------|
E|----------- - ----------0-------------------- - -|
C|----------------0-------------------------- - ---|
G|----------- - ---------- - ----------------------|


A|---------------------- - ----------3------------|
E|----------- - ----------0-------------------- - -|
C|----------------0-------------------------- - ---|
G|----------- - ---------- - ----------------------|


A|---------------------- - ----------2------------|
E|----------- - ----------0-------------------- - -|
C|----------------0-------------------------- - ---|
G|----------- - ---------- - ----------------------|


A|---------------------- - ----------2------------|
E|----------- - ----------0-------------------- - -|
C|----------------0-------------------------- - ---|
G|----------- - ---------- - ----------------------|
```

```
A|------------------------0---------------|
E|----------------1-----------------------|
C|---------3------------------------------|
G|------2---------------------------------|
```

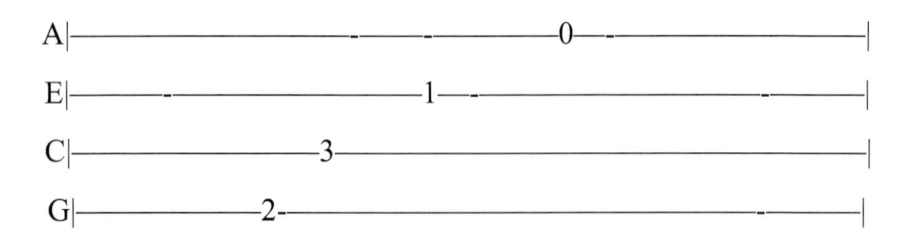

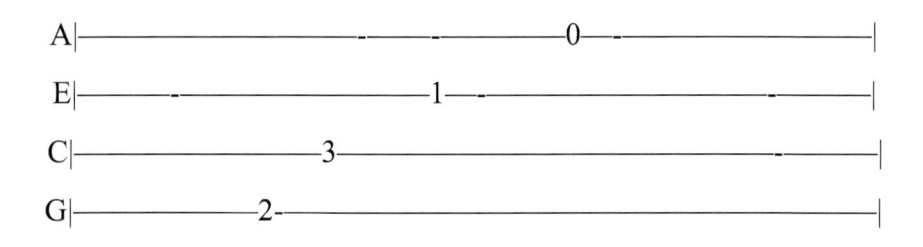

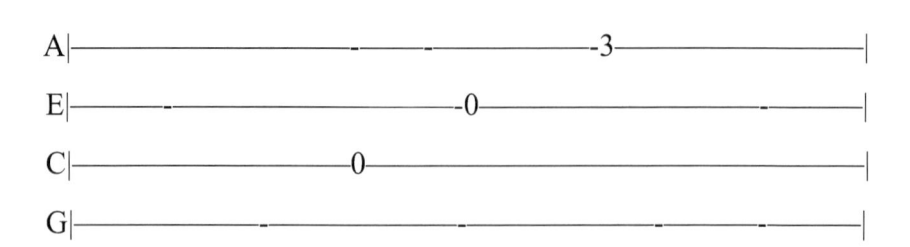

```
A|------------------------0---------------|
E|----------------1-----------------------|
C|---------3------------------------------|
G|------2---------------------------------|
```

```
A|-----------------------3----------------|
E|----------------0-----------------------|
C|---------0------------------------------|
G|----------------------------------------|
```

This chord progression is quite straight forward and with practice, it will become like second nature.

Step 1: Play the C chord twice.

Step 2: Play the C7 chord twice.

Step 3: Play the F7 chord twice.

Step 4: Finish the progression on a single strum of C major.

For the second progression, we will incorporate some fifth chords as well.

C5 C5 G5 G5 F7 F7 C

Again, take your time with this chord progression. It is also in the key of C.

Step 1: Play the C5 chord twice.

Step 2: Play the G5 chord twice. The move might seem hard at first but with time, you'll find this transition much easier.

Step 3: Play the F7 chord twice.

Step 4: Finish the progression on a single strum of C major.

```
A|---------------------------------3---------------|
E|----------------------------3--------------------|
C|-------------------0-----------------------------|
G|-------------0-----------------------------------|


A|---------------------------------3---------------|
E|----------------------------3--------------------|
C|-------------------0-----------------------------|
G|-------------0-----------------------------------|


A|---------------------------------5---------------|
E|----------------------------3--------------------|
C|-------------------2-----------------------------|
G|-------------0-----------------------------------|


A|---------------------------------5---------------|
E|----------------------------3--------------------|
C|-------------------2-----------------------------|
G|-------------0-----------------------------------|
```

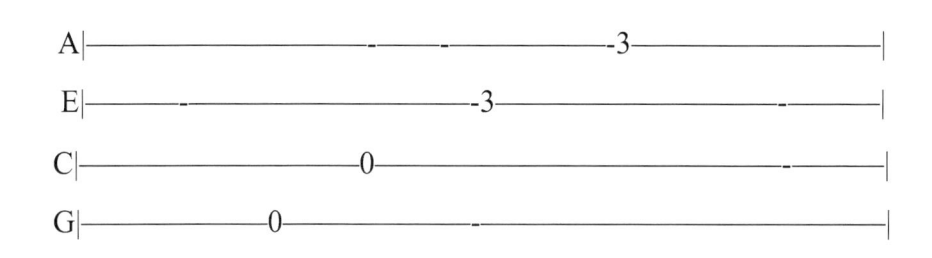

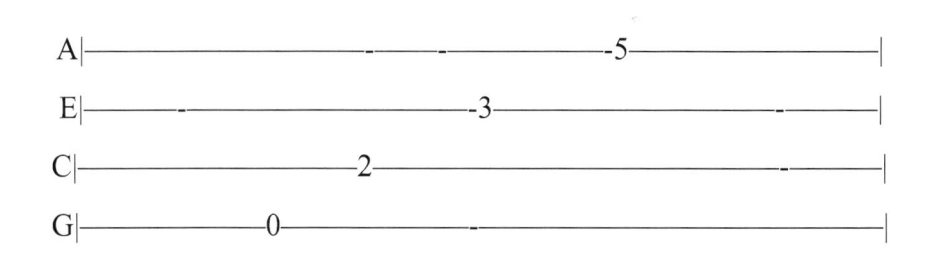

```
A|-------------------------------0-----------------|
E|---------------------1---------------------------|
C|------------3------------------------------------|
G|------2------------------------------------------|


A|-----------------------------3-------------------|
E|----------------------0--------------------------|
C|-------------0-----------------------------------|
G|-------------------------------------------------|
```

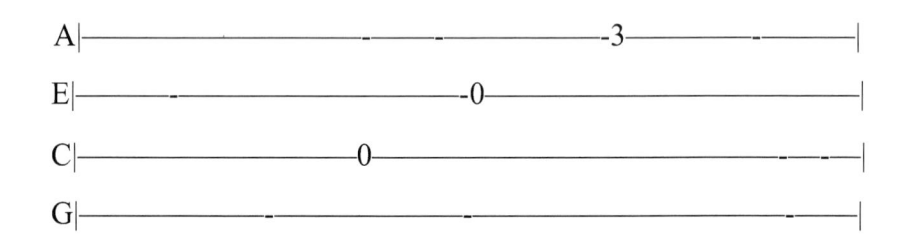

Conclusion

Congratulations for reaching the end. Remember to persist in your practice and go over the exercises and lessons as many times as you need until you feel as though you have mastered each one. Best of luck!

Printed in Great Britain
by Amazon